LENTEN
COOKBOOK

Arestedis Laftsidis

INTRODUCTION

This book was written for those of us who love to cook, but want to prepare something quick and easy during Orthodox Lent. It is certainly not intended to get you through the entire length of time that we fast as Orthodox Christians; more of a go to when you need to make a simple meal. Keeping that in mind, the recipe ideas utilize ingredients, that should be readily available in any large grocery chain and/or local market. The use of a brand name ingredient is not an endorsement; the list of contents for these products was vegan when the recipe was prepared. Please read labels & check for non Lenten ingredients if using a substitute.

Working in and around the concessions & catering businesses (mostly back of the house) I did find time to ask questions, watch and learn from some of the most talented individuals around. After I was finally given the opportunity to work in a restaurant and catering kitchen on the line, I was able to prepare meals efficiently, after a pretty shaky start & well pointed direction. While it has been a while since I have been in the game, I still thoroughly enjoy cooking for small parties, volunteering for food events at my church and, quite frankly, making meals for my father, mother and brother during lent & on feast days.

A quick note about serving sizes. In keeping with the idea that we should only have one modest meal a day during lent, the size range for servings is from hearty to modest (2-3 would be two plates for a hungry couple and three for a smaller, yet filling portion). Also, most dishes should be ready to serve in about an hour, including prep time. All of the equipment used is more than likely in your kitchen (I did use my chef's pan quite a bit, but a non-stick wok with tight fitting lid will work just as well).

Please keep in mind that I am not a professional chef, or food stylist, nor do I take pictures for a living, but there is a color photograph of each dish as prepared on a variety of plates. Hopefully this will give you an idea of what the final product might look like. There is also a notes box under each recipe; I encourage you to make each dish your own adding, removing and adjusting any ingredients that you wish. Not included are phrases, stories and scripture; if you do need guidance during the Lenten periods of our calendar year (or at any other time), reach out to your parish priest so that he can provide you with the direction and/or advice that is required.

Finally, I truly appreciated that you have purchased this book. A portion of the proceeds from every original sale of this book will be donated to charity in memory of loved ones and in prayers for the living. Thank you!

DEDICATION

For everyone that inspired, taught, listened, tested, helped and ate, I thank you from the bottom of my heart. You have all reminded me that one should never give up on a dream and never stop working to achieve it.

For my father, mother & brother, without your love & support this culinary adventure could not have been completed. I will never be able thank you enough.

CONTENTS

<u>VEGETARIAN DISHES</u>

(cheese-fare week)

PASTA CARBONARA

MARGHERITA PIZZA

MACARONI & CHEESE

FRITTATA

STUFFED SHELLS

PASTA CARBONARA w/PEAS – Serves 2 to 3

Pasta with cream and cooked eggs prepared in one pot. Use any choice of pasta to make this dish your own. The heat from the pasta will cook the eggs, so the key is to not to let it cool after draining.

NOTES:

PASTA CARBONARA W/PEAS

Ingredients:

8	ounces	Penne Pasta
1	small	Orange Bell Pepper
2	cloves	Garlic
2	large	Eggs
¼	cup	Half & Half
1	cup	Frozen Peas
½	cup	Romano Cheese (grated)
¼	teasp	Salt
⅛	teasp	Black Pepper

Method:

- Cut the Orange Bell Pepper into a fine dice (about ½ cup) and mince the Garlic, or use a garlic press. Place the pepper in the bottom of the pasta strainer and place in your sink. In a small bowl, beat the Eggs along with the Half & Half, Garlic, Salt & Pepper and set aside.

- Cook the Pasta according to the package directions; with 3 minutes left add the Frozen Peas to the pot. Drain the pasta & peas using the strainer that contains the diced pepper.

- Shake to remove excess water; it's okay to have the pasta a bit "wet" as a little extra water will aid in cooking and make the sauce creamier.

- Dump the pasta and vegetables back into the pot & pour in the egg mixture, along with the Romano Cheese & stir until smooth. If you are concerned about cooking the eggs completely, you can perform this over low heat.

MARGHERITA PIZZA – Serves 3 to 4

This classic Italian pizza is made with Pita bread so it cooks
quickly & is easy to prepare. There are many possibilities for
adding vegetables; keep in mind that with the short baking time
toppings should be pre-cooked.

NOTES:

MARGHERITA PIZZA

Ingredients:

4	each	Pita Bread (pocket-less)
12	ounces	Fresh Mozzarella
1	can	Crushed Tomatoes (14 ounces)
1	teasp	Corn Oil
1	teasp	Oregano (dried)
1	teasp	Sugar
1	teasp	Garlic (granulated)
1	teasp	Salt
$1/_8$	teasp	Black Pepper
4	tablesp	Parmesan Cheese (grated)
8	leaves	Fresh Basil

Method:

- Preheat oven to 450 degrees.
- In a small bowl, stir together the Crushed Tomatoes, Corn Oil, Oregano, Sugar, Garlic, Salt & Black Pepper until combined. Set aside.
- Cut the Mozzarella into ¼ inch slices and then into ¼" cubes. Roll the Basil leaves into a tight tube and cut into thin strips (chiffonade).
- Spread 2 tablespoons of the sauce mixture evenly over each Pita Bread. Add an extra tablespoon if desired. Sprinkle each with a teaspoon of Parmesan, then top each with the cubed cheese using about 11-13 cubes per; no need to make it look even, this is a rustic style pizza. Finally, add the basil to each pita.
- Place two of the prepared pizzas on a cookie sheet and place on the center rack of the oven. Cook for 7-9 minutes, or until the cheese is melted and beginning to bubble. Actual cooking time will depend on your oven (I found it best to cook 2 at a time, instead of all 4 on different racks).
- Remove from oven & allow to cool slightly before serving.
- If you are going to add vegetables (as described on the picture page) try to limit them to 2 and use sparingly.

MACARONI & CHEESE – Serves 2 to 3

Of course any type of pasta can be used in place of elbows. The topping can be left off and you can certainly substitute more grated cheddar instead. Use any sharpness you desire or even white cheddar.

NOTES:

MACARONI AND CHEESE

Ingredients:

2	cups	Elbow Macaroni
¼	cup	Flour (all purpose)
¼	cup	Butter
1 ¼	cup	Whole Milk
½	cup	Half & Half
½	teasp	Dry Mustard
½	teasp	Paprika
½	teasp	Garlic (granulated)
2	cups	Sharp Cheddar Cheese (grated)
2	tablesp	Romano Cheese (grated)
2	tablesp	Bread Crumbs (plain)

Method:

- Preheat oven to 400 degrees. Lightly spray an 8" x 8" glass baking dish with cooking spray and set aside.
- Cook the Elbow Macaroni as directed on the package, subtracting 2 minutes from the total cooking time. Drain and set aside to cool slightly.
- In a large non-stick sauce pot, melt the Butter over low heat. Add the flour and whisk to combine. Slowly stir in the Milk, Half & Half, Dry Mustard, Paprika and Garlic and continue to whisk until smooth.
- Increase the heat to medium and add the Cheddar Cheese, about a half cup at a time and whisk until melted each time. The mixture should be smooth and creamy.
- Remove from heat and stir in the cooked macaroni and mix well to combine. Pour the mixture into the baking dish and spread evenly, if needed. In a small bowl, mix the Parmesan and Bread Crumbs together and sprinkle evenly over the top of the macaroni and cheese.
- Place the pan on the center rack of the oven and bake for 15-20 minutes, or until the topping turns golden brown and cheese begins to bubble along the sides of the pan.

FRITTATA – Serves 2 to 3

Another Italian classic that can be enjoyed at any time of the day. For a little bit of heat use a Pepper Jack cheese to top or Monterey Jack for a milder creamier taste. Depending on your oven, you may need to finish this for a minute or two under the broiler.

NOTES:

FRITTATA

Ingredients:

1	small	Red Bell Pepper
1	small	Green Bell Pepper
2	medium	White Mushrooms
4	ounces	Swiss Cheese
6	large	Eggs
1	tablesp	Half & Half
¼	teasp	Garlic (granulated)
¼	teasp	Onion (grantulated)
½	teasp	Oregano (dried)
¼	teasp	Salt
⅛	teasp	Black Pepper
1	tablesp	Butter
1	tablesp	Canola Oil

Method:

- Preheat oven to 400 degrees.
- Cut the Red Bell Pepper, Green Bell Pepper into a fine dice; there should be about ¼ cup of each. Remove the stem from the Mushrooms, peel the caps and cut into a fine dice to equal about ½ cup. Grate the Swiss cheese, there should be about 1 cup and set aside.
- In a medium sized bowl, beat the Eggs, Half & Half, Garlic, Onion, Oregano, Salt & Pepper until well combined.
- In 8" or 9" oven safe non stick skillet, heat the Butter and Canola Oil over medium-low heat until the butter has melted. Add the vegetables and sauté for 3-4 minutes, or until the peppers have softened and the mushrooms begin to lose volume.
- Pour in the egg mixture and stir until combined, making sure to scrape the sides. Reduce the heat to low and loosely cover with a piece of aluminum foil. Cook for 3-4 minutes, or until the eggs begin to set.
- Remove the foil, sprinkle on the Swiss Cheese and place on the center rack of the oven. Bake for 4-5 minutes, or until the top begins to turn golden brown.

STUFFED SHEELS – Serves 3 to 4

This is a simple version of this dish that can be made quickly if you have all of the ingredients available. Feel free to use pre-grated Mozzarella cheese to save time.

NOTES:

STUFFED SHELLS

Ingredients:

16	jumbo	Pasta Shells
1	can	Crushed Tomatoes (14.5 ounces)
2	tablesp	Canola Oil
½	teasp	Oregano (dried)
2	teasp	Sugar
¼	teasp	Salt
⅛	teasp	Black Pepper
2	large	Eggs
1	tablesp	Basil (dried)
1	teasp	Garlic (granulated)
½	teasp	Onion (granulated)
15	ounces	Ricotta Cheese (part-skim)
1 ½	cups	Mozzarella Cheese (shredded)
1	cup	Parmesan Cheese (grated)

Method:

- Preheat oven to 350 degrees. Cook the Pasta Shells according to the package directions, drain, separate, place on cookie sheet and set aside.
- While the pasta cooks, pour the Crushed Tomatoes, Canola Oil, Oregano, Sugar, Salt & Pepper into a small bowl and whisk until combined. Set aside.
- In a large bowl, beat together the Eggs, Basil, Garlic and Onion for one minute. Add the Ricotta , Mozzarella, and Parmesan cheeses and fold together until well combined.
- Coat the bottom of an 8" x 12" baking dish with half of the tomato mixture (about ¾ of a cup. Fill each of the shells with a tablespoon of the cheese mixture, then evenly divide the remaining cheese amongst the shells.
- Place each shell in the baking dish and spoon the rest of tomato mixture over each shell separately (about 1 teaspoon each).
- Bake for 35-40 minutes on the center rack of the oven, or until the sauce around each shell begins to bubble.

VEGAN BEAN BASED DISHES

BLACK BEAN CHILI

BEANS & GREENS

SPLIT YELLOW PEAS W/CARROTS

SUCCOTASH

STOVE TOP BEANS

FALAFEL

DAHL MAKHANI

WHITE BEAN CASSOULET

VEGAN BLACK BEAN CHILI – Serves 3 to 4

This is a basic chunky chili recipe, so feel free to use any type of canned bean that you like. For heat, add red chili flakes or your favorite hot sauce to taste. If you prefer a looser chili, double the amount of tomato juice or substitute canned tomato sauce for a richer consistency.

NOTES:

BLACK BEAN CHILI

Ingredients:

1	large	White Onion
1	large	Green Bell Pepper
2	stalks	Celery
2	cloves	Garlic
2	tablesp	Corn Oil
1	can	Petite Diced Tomatoes (28 ounces)
1	cup	Tomato Juice
1	teasp	Cumin (ground)
1	teasp	Oregano (dried)
1	teasp	Chili Powder
1	teasp	Paprika
1	teasp	Sugar
1	teasp	Salt
$\frac{1}{8}$	teasp	Black Pepper
1	can	Black Beans (28 ounces)
1	cup	Corn (frozen)

Method:

- Drain & rinse the Black Beans and set aside. Cut the Onion & Green Bell Pepper into a medium dice to equal about 1 cup of each. Cut the Celery into a fine dice to equal about ½ cup. Mince the Garlic cloves, or run through a press.

- In a large sauce pot, heat the Corn Oil over medium heat and add the chopped vegetables. Sauté for 5 minutes, or until they begin to soften. Add the Garlic and continue to sauté for an additional 2 minutes, or until it becomes fragrant.

- Add the Diced Tomatoes, Tomato Juice, Cumin, Oregano, Chili Powder, Paprika, Sugar, Salt, Pepper & Black Beans, stir to combine.

- Increase the heat to high, bring the mixture to a boil, then reduce heat to low, cover and simmer for 15-20 minutes, stirring occasionally.

- Add the Frozen Corn, stir and continue to simmer for 5 more minutes. Remove from heat, uncover and allow to stand for 5 minutes before serving.

BEANS AND GREENS – Serves 2 to 3

This combination of greens is slightly on the bitter side, so the finish with lime juice and sugar can be to taste. Adding a pinch of red pepper flakes, along with the escarole will bring an another layer of flavor. It will be a bit soupy, but the liquid is great mop up with some crusty bread.

NOTES:

BEANS AND GREENS

Ingredients:

2	cans	Butter Beans (15 ounces each)
1	head	Escarole (about 1 pound)
1	bunch	Endive (about 1 pound)
1	large	Yellow Onion
3	cloves	Garlic
2	tablesp	Corn Oil
1 ½	cups	Vegetable Broth
2	teasp	Basil (dried)
2	teasp	Ginger (dried)
1	teasp	Salt
⅛	teasp	Black Pepper
1	tablesp	Sugar
1	tablesp	Lime Juice

Method:

- Drain and rinse the Butter Beans; place half of one can (about 10-12 beans) in a small bowl and mash with a fork until you have a course paste.

- Coarsely chop the Escarole and Endive, discarding the cores and keep each green separate. Thoroughly rinse and dry each, using a salad spinner if available, or pat dry with a clean kitchen towel. The total of greens should be somewhere between 8-12 cups.

- Cut the Onion into a medium dice; total should be about one and one half cups. Mince the Garlic Cloves (or use a press).

- In a large sauté pan, chef's pan or wok heat the Corn Oil over medium heat and add the onion and cook for 3-4 minutes, or until they begin to soften.

- Add the endive and garlic, stir to combine, coating the leaves with any oil and/or juices created by the sauté. Cook uncovered until the leaves begin to wilt, about 3-5 minutes.

- Stir in the escarole, Vegetable Broth, Basil, Ginger, Salt & Pepper and bean paste until well combined. Bring to a boil, reduce to simmer and continue to cook, uncovered, for 10-15 minutes or until the greens have softened. Remove from heat, stir in the Sugar & Lime Juice and serve.

SPILT YELLOW PEAS – Serves 2 to 3

This split yellow pea is in the legume family and prepared to the point of being cooked & not falling apart, as in a split pea soup, makes this a heartier dish.

NOTES:

SPLIT YELLOW PEAS W/CARROTS

Ingredients:

1 ½	cups	Split Yellow Peas (dried)
1	medium	Yellow Onion
1	pound	Baby Cut Fresh Carrots
2	cloves	Garlic
2	tablesp	Corn Oil
3	cups	Vegetable Broth
½	teasp	Sage (rubbed)
½	teasp	Ginger (dried)
½	teasp	Basil (dried)
½	teasp	Salt
2	each	Bay Leaves (dried)

Method:

- Cut the Onion into a small dice, to equal about 1 cup and mince the Garlic Cloves. Rinse & drain the Carrots.
- In a large sauce pot, heat the Corn Oil over medium heat. Add the onion, garlic and Split Yellow Peas and sauté for 3-4 minutes, or until the onions begin to soften, stirring frequently.
- Pour in the Vegetable Broth and add the Sage, Ginger and Salt and stir to combine. Increase the heat to high and bring the mixture to a boil.
- Add the Carrots and Bay Leaves, let the pot come back up to a boil and reduce the heat to medium-low. Cook for 15-20 minutes, uncovered, or until most of the liquid has been absorbed, stirring occasionally. Cover and continue to cook for 10-15 minutes, or until all of the liquid has been absorbed. Remove from heat and let stand, covered for 5 minutes, stir and serve.
- The peas should be firm yet tender.

SUCCOTASH – Serves 2 to 3

There are many versions of this Classic American fare. Here is a
Lenten/vegan take that uses a combination of fresh and frozen
vegetables. It's okay if the vegetables and beans begin to brown
slightly during the cooking process; it adds to the flavor of the
entire dish.

NOTES:

SUCCOTASH

Ingredients:

1	medium	Yellow Onion
1	medium	Zucchini
1	medium	Red Bell Pepper
1	clove	Garlic
2	tablesp	Corn Oil
1	bag	Frozen Lima Beans (16 ounces)
1	cup	Corn (frozen)
1	teasp	Marjoram (dried)
½	teasp	Thyme (dried)
½	teasp	Sage (rubbed)
½	teasp	Salt
⅛	teasp	Black Pepper

Method:

- Cut the Yellow Onion, Zucchini into a small dice to equal about 1 cup of each. Finely dice the Red Bell Pepper, you should yield about ½ cup. Mince the Garlic clove.
- In a large skillet, or chef's pan, heat the Corn Oil over medium heat and add the onions. Sauté for 7-10 minutes or until they begin to slightly brown and caramelize. Stir in the zucchini and red pepper and cook for 3-4 minutes, or until they begin to soften.
- Add the Frozen Lima Beans, Frozen Corn, garlic, Marjoram, Thyme, Sage, Salt and Pepper and stir to combine thoroughly. Pour in ¼ cup of water and continue to stir. Reduce to the heat to medium-low and cook for 8-10 minutes, or until the beans and corn have heated through and are tender.
- You may need to add a tablespoon or two more of water, but there should be enough moisture from the frozen vegetables to steam them.

STOVETOP BEANS – Serves 3 to 4

Here is a quick recipe that has the taste of slow cooked baked beans. While generally any white bean will work, the best flavor comes from pinto beans.

NOTES:

STOVETOP BEANS

Ingredients:

2	cans	Pinto Beans (28 ounces each)
1	large	Yellow Onion
3	cloves	Garlic
2	tablesp	Corn Oil
½	teasp	Salt
⅛	teasp	Black Pepper
½	cup	Dark Brown Sugar
⅓	cup	Ketchup
2	teasp	Cider Vinegar
2	teasp	Dry Mustard
1	teasp	Cumin

Method:

- Drain and rinse the Pinto Beans and set aside. Dissolve the Dark Brown Sugar in 1 cup of hot water and set aside.
- Cut the Onion into a large dice to equal about 1 ½ cups. Lightly crush the Garlic, trying to leave the cloves as whole as possible.
- In a medium stock pot, heat the Corn Oil over medium heat and add the onions, garlic, Salt & Pepper and cook for 4-5 minutes, or until they begin to soften & turn fragrant, stirring frequently.
- Add the pinto beans, brown sugar mixture, Ketchup, Cider Vinegar, Dry Mustard, and Cumin and stir until well combined.
- Reduce the heat to low, cover and continue to cook for 30-35 minutes, stirring frequently. If the beans become dry, add up to ¾ of a cup, a quarter cup at a time during cooking.

FALAFEL – Serves 2 to 3

A Middle Eastern snack food that has become very popular and is quite easy to prepare. Serve with rice, or a salad to make this a complete meal. This recipe can be easily doubled to feed a small crowd.

NOTES:

FALAFEL

Ingredients:

1	can	Chick Peas (28 ounces)
½	bunch	Curley Parsley
1	tablesp	Lime Juice
½	cup	All Purpose Flour
2	teasp	Baking Powder
2	teasp	Garlic (granulated)
1	teasp	Onion (granulated)
2	teasp	Cumin (ground)
2	teasp	Coriander (ground)
½	teasp	Salt
2	cups	Canola Oil

Method:

- Drain and rinse the Chick Peas. Coarsely chop the Parsley to equal about 1 cup. Put both of these items into a food processor along with the Lime Juice and pulse until the mixture becomes crumbly; be sure to scrape down the sides & check that there are no whole peas or large pieces. Be careful not to over process and turn it into a paste.

- In a small bowl, combine the Flour, Baking Powder, Granulated Garlic & Onion, Cumin, Coriander & Salt and mix together.

- Transfer the processed chick pea mixture to a large bowl and add the dry ingredients. Using your hand, or a rubber spatula, mix everything together until the mixture begins to tighten and form a slightly loose dough. Additional flour may be added, a tablespoon at a time, if needed.

- Roll the falafel into small balls, slightly larger than a golf ball (there should be a total of 10) and then flatten into patties that are about ½ inch thick and set aside to rest for 5 minutes.

- While the falafel rests, heat one cup of the Canola Oil, in a 10" skillet over medium-high heat. Once the oil has come up to temperature, place half of the patties in and cook for 4-5 minutes on the first side, or until the edges begin to turn brown and form a crust. Flip and cook on the other side for 3-4 minutes. Remove and drain on paper towels. Repeat the process with the remaining falafels, add more oil if needed.

DAL MAKHANI (creamy lentils) – Serves 3 to 4

This dish is a northern Indian stew that is normally prepared using milk and clarified butter. In this vegan version, coconut milk is substituted along with corn oil. The use of canned lentils & beans makes it easy to prepare.

NOTES:

DAL MAKHANI

Ingredients:

1	medium	Red Onion
1	medium	Plum Tomato
3	cans	Lentils (14 ounces each)
1	can	Dark Red Kidney Beans (15 ounces)
1	cup	Coconut Milk
1	teasp	Ginger (dry)
1	teasp	Garlic (granulated)
½	teasp	Cumin
½	teasp	Chili Powder
½	teasp	Curry Powder
1	teasp	Coriander (ground)
1	teasp	Salt
¼	teasp	Black Pepper
2	tablesp	Corn Oil

Method:

- Finely dice the Red Onion and cut the Plum Tomato into a medium dice; there should a cup of onion & ½ cup tomato.
- Drain and rinse 2 cans of the Lentils and the can of Kidney beans; reserve 2 tablespoons of the kidney beans.
- Place the rinsed lentils & beans in a food processor, along with the tomato, Coconut Milk, Ginger, Garlic, Cumin, Chili Powder, Curry Powder, Coriander, Salt & Pepper and process until smooth, about 4-5 minutes; scrape down the sides half way through.
- While the bean mixture is processing, drain and rinse the last can of lentils and set aside with the reserved kidney beans.
- Heat the Corn Oil over medium heat, add the onion and sauté for 2-3 minutes, or until it becomes fragrant. Add the processed lentils and beans and ½ cup of water and stir until well combined. Reduce heat to low, cover and simmer for 25-30 minutes, stirring frequently, until the stew has become thick and creamy.

WHITE BEAN CASSOULET – Serves 2 to 3

A French dish that is usually made with a variety of meats and
slow cooked. In this version, mushrooms are substituted and
root vegetables add a new flavor twist.

NOTES:

WHITE BEAN CASSOULET

Ingredients:

1	medium	Yellow Onion
2	medium	Parsnip
1	small	Turnip
2	cloves	Garlic
8	ounces	White Mushrooms
3	tablesp	Corn Oil
2	cups	Vegetable Broth
2	cans	White Cannellini Beans
½	teasp	Basil (dried)
¼	teasp	Thyme (dried)
½	teasp	Coriander (ground)
½	teasp	Tarragon (dried)
½	teasp	Salt
⅛	teasp	Black Pepper
2	tablesp	Bread Crumbs (plain)
1	teasp	Garlic (granulated)
1	teasp	Onion (granulated)

Method:

- Preheat the oven to 375 degrees and lightly coat an 8" x 8" baking dish with cooking spray.
- Cut the Onion into a fine dice to equal about ½ cup. Cut the Parsnip & Turnip into a small dice to equal about 1 ½ cups of parsnip & about ½ cup of turnip. Mince the Garlic cloves.
- Remove the stems from the Mushrooms and peel the caps. Drain and rinse the White Beans & set aside.
- In a large stock pot, heat the Corn Oil over medium heat. Add the onion, parsnip, turnip, garlic, Basil, Thyme, Coriander, Tarragon, Salt & Pepper and sauté for 5-7 minutes, or until the mushrooms begin to lose volume, stirring frequently.
- Pour in the Vegetable Broth & add the White Beans, increase the heat to high, stir and bring to a boil. Remove from heat.
- Ladle the mixture into the baking dish, place on the center rack of the oven and bake, uncovered, for 45 minutes.
- Combine the Bread Crumbs, Garlic & Onion in a small bowl. Remove the beans from the oven, carefully stir & sprinkle the crumb mixture over the top. Bake for an additional 15 minutes, or until the liquid has been absorbed.

VEGAN VEGETABLE BASED DISHES

FRENCH ONION SOUP

POSOLE VERDE

CHEF'S SALAD

SPANAKORIZO

GAZPACHO

PORTOBELLO MUSHROOM BURGER

BAKED VEGEATBLE PACKETS

VEGETABLE MASALA

HASH POTATOES

BRIAM

SPAGHETTI SQUASH

SWEET POTATO STEW

GUMBO

ENSALADILLA

FRENCH ONION SOUP – Serves 3 to 4

Traditionally topped with a crouton & melted cheese, this lighter, vegan version tastes just as good on its own. Using a store purchased, or home made vegetable stock, in place of the broth in this recipe will add an even deeper richer flavor.

NOTES:

FRENCH ONION SOUP

Ingredients:

3	pounds	Spanish Onions
3	tablesp	Corn Oil
3	cloves	Garlic
6	cups	Vegetable Broth
1	teasp	Tarragon (dried)
1	tablesp	Soy Sauce
1	tablesp	Gravy Master® Liquid Seasoning
2	each	Bay Leaves
1/8	teasp	Black Pepper

Method:

- Peel the Spanish Onions, trim off the tops & root end and cut in half lengthwise. With the flat side down, cut the onion into ½ inch thick slices (or half moons). Mince the Garlic , or use a press.

- In a large stock pot, or Dutch oven, heat the Corn Oil over medium–low heat add the onions. Sauté for 10 minutes uncovered, then 10 minutes covered, and then 10 minutes uncovered again, stirring frequently during this process. The onions should begin to caramelize during the final 10 minutes.

- Add the Garlic, stir and sauté for 1-2 minutes. Pour in the Vegetable Broth, Soy Sauce, Gravy Master® and add in the Tarragon, Bay Leaves & Black Pepper.

- Increase the heat, bring the soup to a boil, then reduce to low and simmer, covered, for 25-30 minutes. Remember to stir once or twice during this last stage of cooking.

POSOLE VERDE – Serves 2 to 3

This is a "green" version of a traditional tomato based Mexican soup. All of the ingredients should be available at your local supermarket in this easy to prepare & hearty recipe.

NOTES:

POSOLE VERDE

Ingredients:

1	medium	Poblano Pepper
2	small	Tomatillos
3	cloves	Garlic
¼	bunch	Cilantro
1	medium	Yellow Onion
2	tablesp	Corn Oil
4	cups	Vegetable Broth (divided)
1	can	Hominy (28 ounces)
2	teasp	Oregano (dried)
¼	head	Savoy Cabbage
1	small	Avocado

Method:

- Cut the Poblano in half, remove the seeds & white ribs and coarsely chop in ½ inch pieces (about ⅓ cup). Remove the papery husk from the Tomatillos & wash off any waxy residue under warm running water. Remove the stem core and cut into a small dice (about ½ cup). Peel the Garlic cloves; finely chop the Cilantro to equal about ¼ cup. Cut the Onion into a medium dice (1 cup) and finely shred the Cabbage to equal about 1 cup (tightly packed).
- Drain & rinse the Hominy under cold water. Set aside.
- In a blender, or small food processor, process the poblano, tomatillo, garlic, cilantro & 1 cup of the vegetable broth for 1-2 minutes, or until smooth.
- In a medium stock pot, heat the Corn Oil over medium heat. Add the onions and Oregano and sauté for 3-4 minutes, or until the onions begin to soften & become fragrant. Pour in the processed mixture and cook until it has reduced by about a third (5-7 minutes), stirring occasionally.
- Add the remaining vegetable broth, increase the heat, bring to a boil, reduce to simmer, cover and cook for 10-15 minutes, or until the hominy begins to soften slightly.
- Remove the pot from the heat, add the Cabbage, cover and allow to stand for 5 minutes. Server with an Avocado wedge.

CHEF'S SALAD – Serves 2 to 3

Of course, the contents of this salad are up to you as the recipe here is for the dressing. Including a fruit and nut, such as apple & walnuts will make this more of a meal.

NOTES:

CHEF'S SALAD

Ingredients:

2	bags	Mixed Salad Greens (12 ounces each)
1	pint	Cherry Tomatoes
1	medium	English Cucumber (seedless)
½	cup	Blueberries
½	cup	Almonds (slivered)
¼	cup	Balsamic Vinegar
2	teasp	Sugar
½	teasp	Oregano (dried)
1	teasp	Garlic (granulated)
½	teasp	Onion (granulated)
¼	teasp	Salt
⅛	teasp	Black Pepper
1	teasp	Dijon Mustard
1	teasp	Lemon Juice
¾	cup	Canola Oil

Method:

- Cut the Cucumber in half length-wise and then into half moons.
- Divide the Salad Greens, Cherry Tomatoes, Blueberries, Almonds and cucumbers equally.
- Pour the Balsamic Vinegar into a bowl large enough to use a whisk and add the Sugar, Oregano, Garlic, Onion, Salt, Pepper, Dijon Mustard and Lemon Juice and whisk until combined.
- While continuing to whisk, slowly drizzle in the Canola Oil. The dressing should emulsify and bring everything together into a smooth dressing. If you do prepare the dressing in advance, give it a quick whisk before serving if the oil has separated from the rest of the ingredients.
- In addition to using your choice of fruits, vegetables & nuts, any type of vinegar (such as Cider, or White) will work just as well. Keep in mind that Wine Vinegar should only be used on days permitted during lent.

SPANAKORIZO (Spinach & Rice) – Serves 2 to 3

A classic Greek dish prepared with fresh spinach, rice and
tomato sauce, that is slow simmered, lightly seasoned and
finished with lemon.

NOTES:

SPANAKORIZO (SPINACH & RICE)

Ingredients:

2	bags	Spinach (10 ounces each)
1	large	Yellow Onions
2	cloves	Garlic
1/3	cup	Corn Oil
1	cup	White Rice (long grain)
1	can	Tomato Sauce (8 ounces)
2	cups	Vegetable Broth
1/4	teasp	Nutmeg (ground)
1/4	teasp	Allspice (ground)
1/4	teasp	Salt
1/8	teasp	Black Pepper
2	tablesp	Lemon Juice

Method:

- Trim the stems from the Spinach, wash thoroughly and set aside to drain. Cut the Yellow Onion into a medium dice to equal about 1 ½ cups. Mince the Garlic cloves, or run through a press.
- In a large frying pan, or chef's pan, heat the Corn Oil over medium heat; add the onion and sauté for 3-5 minutes, or until they begin to soften and start to turn translucent. Stir in the White Rice & Garlic and continue to sauté for 2-3 minutes, or until the garlic becomes fragrant, stirring occasionally.
- Add the spinach, stir to coat and allow to cook for 3-4 minutes or the leaves begin to wilt (you may need to perform this step in batches, depending on the size of the pan being used).
- Stir in the Tomato Sauce, Vegetable Broth, Nutmeg, Allspice, Salt & Pepper until well combined. Increase the heat, bring to a boil, then reduce heat to low and simmer, covered, and cook for 15-20 minutes, or until the rice is done. Be sure to stir occasionally, so that the spinach does not scorch.
- Remove from heat, stir in the Lemon Juice and serve.

GAZPACHO – Serves 3 to 4

A Spanish chilled soup that can be easily prepared and mostly made during the warmer summer months. Accompanied by a loaf of crusty bread, this dish can certainly eat like a meal.

NOTES:

GAZPACHO

Ingredients:

2	medium	Red Bell Pepper
1	large	Red Onion
1	large	English Cucumber (seedless)
3	large	Tomatoes
1	clove	Garlic
2	tablesp	Lime Juice
1	tablesp	Cider Vinegar
1	teasp	Basil (dried)
½	teasp	Oregano (dried)
2	teasp	Sugar
½	teasp	Salt
¼	teasp	Black Pepper
3	cups	Tomato Juice (divided)
1	small	Fresh Chive (bunch)

Method:

- Peel the Cucumber, cut in half length-wise and scrape out the soft center. Cut the vegetables into a small dice to equal the following approximate quantities. Red Bell Pepper – 1 cup, Red Onion – 1 ½ cups, Cucumber – 1 ½ cups, Tomatoes – 3 cups. Mince the Garlic clove. Reserve up to 1 ½ cups total of all of the vegetables for the last step.

- Place the un-reserved vegetables in a 10 cup food processor, along with the Lime Juice, Cider Vinegar, Basil, Oregano, Sugar, Salt, Pepper and 2 cups of the Tomato Juice. Pulse the mixture for 45-60 seconds, or until it begins to froth and the vegetables have been broken down into very small pieces. Be careful not to over process this into a juice; a consistency of thick marinara would be perfect.

- Pour the processed vegetables into a large bowl, add the reserved vegetables and the remaining tomato juice. Stir to combine, cover and refrigerate for at least 1 hour, or even overnight.

- Mince the Chives to equal about ¼ cup and stir in just before serving.

PORTOBELLO MUSHROOM "BURGER" – Serves 4

Cooking the Portobello mushroom on a barbeque grill, outdoors (if possible) or on an open Panini press gives this sandwich a much better taste. Toppings in this recipe are basic, so feel free to add ketchup, pickles, etc. as desired.

NOTES:

PORTOBELLO MUSHROOM "BURGER"

Ingredients:

4	large	Portobello Mushrooms
½	cup	Canola Oil
½	cup	Balsamic Vinegar
1	teasp	Garlic (granulated)
1	teasp	Onion (granulated)
2	teasp	Basil (dried)
½	teasp	Salt
¼	teasp	Black Pepper
½	teasp	Sugar
4	each	Onion Rolls
4	leaves	Green Leaf Lettuce
1	small	Tomato
1	small	Red Onion

Method:

- Remove the stems from the Portobello Mushrooms and discard. Using a damp, clean kitchen towel, wipe the tops of the mushrooms to remove any dirt. With the tip of a sharp knife, score the tops forming ½" squares, being careful not to cut all the way through. Set aside.

- In a small bowl, whisk together the Canola Oil, Balsamic Vinegar, Garlic, Onion, Basil, Salt, Black Pepper and Sugar until combined.

- Place the mushroom caps, tops down, in a pan large enough for them to lay flat, pour over the marinade and lightly rub it into each cap.. Cover with plastic wrap and allow to stand at room temperature for 25-30 minutes. Alternately, you can use a zipper bag for this step, but be careful not to break the mushrooms.

- Heat a large grill pan over medium high heat and place the mushrooms, cap side up first, cooking for 5-7 minutes per side, or until they soften slightly. If you are using a Panini press, as suggested on the previous page, be sure to leave it open, as closing it on the mushrooms will squeeze out the juices. If you are using a frying pan, the caps will tend to steam after the flip resulting in a softer texture but still will taste great.

BAKED VEGETABLE PACKETS – Serves 4

Here is an outdoor summer side dish that can made into an indoor meal. Precut foil packets can be used, but it's just as easy to make them from regular rolled foil. Use your outdoor grill, if available to keep the heat out of the kitchen.

NOTES:

BAKED VEGETABLE PACKETS

Ingredients:

8	small	Red Potatoes (about 1 pound)
12	each	Baby Cut Carrots (about ½ pound)
8	each	Cherry Tomatoes
1	ear	Fresh Corn
8	each	Brussel Sprouts
1	small	Red Onion
½	cup	Corn Oil
2	teasp	Soy Sauce
1	teasp	Garlic (granulated)
½	teasp	Basil (dried)
½	teasp	Sugar
¼	teasp	Salt
¼	teasp	Black Pepper

Method:

- Preheat oven to 375 degrees. Cut the Red Onion into a fine dice to equal about ½ cup.

- Scrub the Red Potatoes under cold running water to remove any loose dirt (or peel if desired), then cut each one in half. Peel the husk off of the Corn and remove all of the silk. And cut into slices with about 2-3 rows of kernels on each.

- In a bowl large enough to hold all of the vegetables, whisk together the Corn Oil, minced onion, Soy Sauce, Garlic, Basil, Sugar, Salt & Pepper until combined. Add the vegetables and toss until coated. Rest at room temperature for 15-20 minutes.

- Cut four pieces of foil from a 12 inch wide roll that are approximately 24 inches long. Fold them in half, creating 12" by 12" double layered squares.

- Stir the vegetables one last time and divide them equally between each of the four squares, placing them in the center. Drizzle any remaining marinade over each of the piles of vegetables.

- Grab opposite sides of the foil, using the folded side as one of them and connect them with one ½ inch fold-over. Seal the ends with a couple of ½" fold-overs. Don't wrap too tight, leave a bit of room for expansion.

- Place the packets on a cookie sheet, on the center rack of the oven and cook for 35-40 minutes.

VEGETABLE MASALA – Serves 3 to 4

This is a slightly spicy Indian dish that you'll need a good Garam Masala to prepare, that should be available at your local market in the ethnic food aisle. It comes together quickly after all of the vegetable prep.

NOTES:

VEGETABLE MASALA

Ingredients:

1	head	Cauliflower (small, about 1 pound)
2	medium	White Potatoes (about 1 pound)
2	medium	Carrots
1	large	Yellow Pepper
1	medium	White Onion
3	cloves	Garlic
2	tablesp	Corn Oil
½	teasp	Salt
1 ½	teasp	Garam Maslala
½	teasp	Ginger (dried)
½	cup	Tomato Juice

Method:

- Core the Cauliflower and cut into medium sized florets, there should be a total of about 5-6 cups. Scrub the White Potatoes under cold running water (or peel if desired) and cut into a large dice. Cut the Carrots & Yellow Bell Pepper into ½ inch chunks and the White Onion into a small dice (about 1 cup). Mince the Garlic, or run through a press.

- In a large frying pan, or chef's pan (make sure you have a tight fitting lid for either), heat the Corn Oil over medium heat and sauté the potatoes, onion and carrots, along with the Salt for 5-7 minutes, or until the onion begins to soften.

- Add the cauliflower, pepper, garlic and cook for 5 minutes, stirring frequently. Stir in the Garam Masala, Ginger, Tomato Juice and ½ cup of water until well combined. Cover and cook for 20-25 minutes, or until the liquid is almost all absorbed and the potatoes are tender.

- Stir the mixture frequently, checking for moisture; there should be enough liquid between the tomato sauce and water to steam the vegetables, but if more is needed add ¼ cup water at a time, stirring well after each addition.

HASH POTATOES – Serves 3 to 4

A traditional breakfast side that can be enjoyed as a main course.
The Yukon Gold potatoes add a naturally buttery taste and the
skins left on make this a rustic dish, but Russet potatoes will
work just as well.

NOTES:

HASH BROWNED POTATOES

Ingredients:

4	medium	Yukon Gold Potatoes
1	cup	Vegetable Broth
1	large	Spanish onion
1	medium	Red Bell Pepper
3	tablesp	Corn Oil
2	cloves	Garlic
1	tablesp	Tarragon (dried)
1	tablesp	Sugar
½	teasp	Salt
¼	teasp	Black Pepper

Method:

- Scrub the Yukon Potatoes under cold running water to remove any loose dirt (or peel if desired). Cut into a large dice to equal roughly 5-6 cups.

- Cut the Spanish Onion into a large dice, about 1 ½ cups, and cut the Red Bell Pepper into a small dice , about 1 cup. Mince the Garlic cloves.

- In a large chef's pan, or large frying pan, bring the Vegetable Broth to a boil, add the potatoes, bring back up to a boil, reduce heat to medium and cook, uncovered, for 5-7 minutes, or until the broth has been absorbed and the potatoes are almost cooked. Remove from the pan and set aside.

- Rinse out the pan, wipe clean and dry completely. Reheat the pan over medium heat, add the Corn Oil, Onion, Garlic, Tarragon, Salt & Black Pepper and sauté for 2-3 minutes, or until the onions begin to soften.

- Add the potatoes and Sugar and mix well to combine all of the ingredients. Let the hash cook, undisturbed for 3-5 minutes, or until the potatoes begin to turn golden brown & a light crust forms on the bottom.

- Add the Red Bell Pepper and cook for an additional 2-3 minutes, stirring frequently.

BRIAM (roasted vegetables) – Serves 3 to 4

This is a Greek version of Ratatouille, oven roasted vegetables that can be enjoyed hot out of the oven, at room temperature or even cold as a salad. Traditionally made with olive oil, corn oil is substituted in this recipe.

NOTES:

BRIAM (ROASTED VEGETABLES)

Ingredients:

2	medium	Yellow Zucchini (summer squash)
2	medium	Green Bell Pepper
1	large	Eggplant
8	small	Red Potatoes
1	large	Red Onion
1	can	Plum Tomatoes (28 ounces)
½	cup	Corn Oil
1	tablesp	Oregano (dried)
1	teasp	Basil (dried)
1	teasp	Garlic (granulated)
1	teasp	Salt
¼	teasp	Black Pepper

Method:

- Preheat oven to 400 degrees.
- The total weight of each vegetable should be about 1 pound, except for the eggplant which should be about 2. No need to peel any of them, except the onion (and removing the top and seeds from the pepper, of course) , just be sure to wash each one thoroughly. The peels will actually help them hold their shape.
- Cut the Zucchini into ½ inch disks, the Green Bell Pepper into 1 inch chunks, the Eggplant into ½" cubes, the Potatoes into quarters, and the Red Onion into a large dice.
- Place all of the cut vegetables in a large roasting pan (12" x 18" was used for this preparation), pour in the Corn Oil and mix well until all of the vegetables are coated (don't be afraid to use your hands).
- Add the Canned Tomatoes, un-drained, Oregano, Basil, Garlic, Salt and Black Pepper and mix again until well combined.
- Bake on the center rack of the oven, uncovered, for 60-90 minutes. Remove from the oven at least twice during the cooking process and carefully stir trying not to break down any of the vegetables. The total cooking time will depend on the size of your cuts and your oven. Serve as suggested on the previous page.

SPAGHETTI SQUASH – Serves 3 to 4

A winter vegetable that is available year-round, that when cooked resembles spaghetti and has a slightly sweet taste. Toping it with this sauté balances out the flavor and creates a sweet & sour contrast.

NOTES:

SPAGHETTI SQUASH

Ingredients:

1	large	Spaghetti Squash (about 3 pounds)
2	cloves	Garlic
1	medium	Red Onion
1	small	Red Bell Pepper
6	ounces	Marinated Artichoke Hearts (jar or canned)
¼	cup	Green Salad Olives (jarred)
½	bunch	Parsley (curly)
½	teasp	Basil (dried)
½	cup	Golden Raisins
2	tablesp	Canola Oil
⅛	teasp	Black Pepper
½	cup	Vegetable Broth

Method:

- Preheat oven to 450 degrees.
- Cut the Spaghetti Squash in half, length-wise, and scoop out the soft center strands and seeds & discard them. Lightly spray the inside with cooking spray and place both halves into a baking dish, cut side down and bake for 30-40 minutes; the skin will begin to turn light brown and should be easily pierced with a toothpick when done. Remove from oven and allow to cool at room temperature until it can be easily handled.
- Mince the Garlic, or run through a press, cut the Red Onion into a small dice, equaling about 1 cup & the Red Bell Pepper into a fine dice equaling about ½ cup. Rinse the Artichoke Hearts and coarsely chop into a small dice, and rinse the Olives. Mince the Parsley to equal about ¼ cup.
- In a medium non-stick skillet, heat the Canola Oil over medium heat and add the onion, bell pepper, Golden Raisins, artichoke, olives, Basil and Black Pepper and sauté for 5-7 minutes, or until the onion begins to caramelize, stirring frequently. Increase the heat to high and pour in the Vegetable Broth and cook for 5-7 minutes, or until the liquid has evaporated. Remove from heat.
- With a large fork, scrape out the flesh of the squash into a large bowl; it should come out in thin strands.
- Divide into servings and top with the sauté.

SWEET POTATO STEW – Serves 3 to 4

This version of a west African dish is meatless and prepared
using one pot. The peanut butter adds a crunchy texture and
acts a thickener. The Chili flakes are optional, but do add just
enough heat to this hearty stew.

NOTES:

SWEET POTATO STEW

Ingredients:

3	medium	Sweet Potatoes (about 2 lbs)
1	pound	Fresh Green Beans
1	medium	Red Onion
2	cloves	Garlic
2	tablesp	Canola Oil
2	cups	Vegetable Broth
1	teasp	Curry Powder
½	teasp	Ginger (dried)
¼	teasp	Cinnamon (ground)
½	teasp	Salt
⅛	teasp	Red Chili Flakes
1	can	Diced Tomatoes (28 ounces)
¼	bunch	Cilantro
½	teasp	Ginger (dried)
⅔	cups	Crunchy Peanut Butter

Method:

- Peel the Sweet Potatoes and cut into 1 inch chunks. Trim both ends of the Green Beans and cut into 1 inch long pieces. Cut the Red Onion into a medium dice, equaling about 1 cup. Mince the Garlic. Mince the Cilantro to equal about ½ cup.

- In a large stock pot, heat the Canola Oil over medium heat, add the sweet potato & onion and sauté for 3-4 minutes, or until the onions begin to soften, stirring frequently. Add the garlic, stir and cook for an additional minute.

- Increase the heat to high, pour in the Vegetable Broth, Curry Powder, Ginger, Cinnamon, Salt, Red Chili Flakes & Canned Tomatoes and stir until well combined. Once it comes to a boil, reduce heat to medium-low, cover and cook for 25-30 minutes, or until the potatoes are tender, but not falling apart. Stir the stew frequently; it will be a bit runny.

- Reduce the heat to low, add the Peanut Butter and gently fold, being careful not to break apart to potatoes. Fold in the cilantro, remove from heat, allow to cool slightly before serving.

GUMBO – Serves 2 to 3

A vegan preparation of a classic southern dish. Upgrade this to a shrimp gumbo by adding defrosted cooked shrimp during the last 5 minutes of cooking time to heat them through. Carefully and slowly cook the roux in step 2; burning the flour in this step will result in a bitter after taste.

NOTES:

GUMBO – (VEGAN)

Ingredients:

⅓	cup	Corn Oil
⅓	cup	Flour (all purpose)
2	stalks	Celery
1	large	Yellow Onion
2	medium	Green Bell Pepper
2	cloves	Garlic
1	teasp	Oregano (dried)
1	teasp	Paprika
½	teasp	Cumin (ground)
½	teasp	Coriander (ground)
½	teasp	Rosemary (dried)
½	teasp	Salt
⅛	teasp	Black Pepper
3	each	Bay Leaves
1	bag	Frozen Okra (16 ounces - sliced)
2	cups	Vegetable Broth

Method:

- Cut the Celery into quarter inch slices, and the Yellow Onion and Green Pepper into a medium dice. There should be about one cup of each. Mince the Garlic clove.

- Heat a large stock pot over medium-low heat. Add the Corn Oil and Flour and whisk until combined and all of the lumps are gone. Cook for 15-20 minutes (even up to 30), or until the color turns the color of milk chocolate, whisking frequently. Once the desired color is reached, stir in the celery, onion and green peppers, mix well, coating the vegetables with the roux, increase the heat to medium & sauté for 5-7 minutes, stirring frequently.

- Add in the Oregano, Paprika, Cumin, Coriander, Rosemary, Salt & Black Pepper and stir to combine well. Cook for 1-2 minutes.

- Mix in the Frozen Okra, Garlic and continue to cook for 4-5 minutes, or until the okra begins to defrost and releases its seed pod sticky substance.

- Stir in the Vegetable Broth & Bay Leaves, increase heat to boil, reduce to medium and simmer 15-20 minutes, or until the seeds begin to release from the okra, stir occasionally. Remove from heat, remove the bay leaves and let stand for 5 minutes..

ENSALADILLA – Serves 2 to 3

This summer favorite in Spain, sometimes referred to as Russian Potato salad, has been updated to a vegan version, and tastes great anytime of the year.

NOTES:

ENSALADILLA

Ingredients:

3	medium	Red Potatoes (about 2 pounds total)
1	pound	Fresh Green Beans
1	medium	Red Bell Pepper
1	medium	Yellow Onion
1	small	Fennel Bulb
1	medium	Carrot
1	clove	Garlic
2	teasp	Yellow Mustard (prepared)
1	teasp	Honey
2	teasp	Lemon Juice
½	teasp	Salt
¼	teasp	Ginger (ground)
⅔	cup	Corn Oil
2	tablesp	Dill Relish

Method:

- Bring 2 quarts of water to a boil in a large stock pot over high heat. While it comes to temperature, prepare the vegetables.

- Peel the Red Potatoes and cut into ½" cubes. Trim both ends of the Green Beans and cut into half inch long pieces. Trim the green stalks from the Fennel Bulb, and discard them. Finely dice the bulb and the Yellow Onion, to equal about ¾ cups each. Cut the Red Bell Pepper into a small dice, to equal about 1 cup and shred the Carrot to equal about ½ cup.

- When the water comes to a boil, add the potatoes and boil for 7-8 minutes, or until they start to become tender. Add the green beans and continue boiling for 4-5 minutes or until they are cooked, but still crisp and the potatoes are fork tender. Drain and rinse under cold running water for 4-5 minutes, or until they are cool to the touch.

- In a large bowl, whisk together the garlic, Yellow Mustard, Honey, Lemon Juice, Salt, and Ginger until well combined. Slowly drizzle in the Corn Oil, while continuing to whisk until the dressing emulsifies.

- Fold in the potatoes, green beans, bell pepper, onion, fennel, carrot and Dill Relish until coated. Cover and refrigerate for at least 1 hour. Stir and serve.

VEGAN GRAIN & PASTA BASED DISHES

CHOW MEIN "NOODLES"

TABBOULEH

RICE PILAF

PASTA PUTTENESCA

COUS COUS

BROWN RICE & MUSHROOMS

STUFFED PEPPERS

KASHA

PUERTO RICAN RICE

CHOW MEIN "noodles"– Serves 2 to 3

For the "noodle" part in this dish, whole wheat spaghetti is used making this not only vegan for lent, but a healthier option to carry out food. It's simple to prepare with oyster sauce, that should be available in the Asian section of your local market.

NOTES:

CHOW MEIN "NOODLES"

Ingredients:

8	ounces	Whole Wheat Spaghetti
1	small	Yellow Onion
2	stalks	Celery
2	small	Carrots
¼	head	Green Cabbage
2	cloves	Garlic
1	cup	Fresh Bean Sprouts
2	tablesp	Oyster Sauce
1	cup	Vegetable Broth
2	teasp	Corn Starch
2	tablesp	Canola oil

Method:

- Cut the Yellow Onion in half, from stem to root and then into thin slices to equal about ½ cup. Slice the Celery into thin slices, to equal about ¾ of a cup & shred the Carrot using a grater, also equaling about ¾ if a cup. Thinly shred the Cabbage, removing the core. There should be about 1 tightly packed cup. Mince the Garlic, or run through a garlic press. Rinse the Bean Sprouts, drain and set aside. Having all of these ingredients at hand will make the stir fry go a lot more smoothly.

- Cook the Spaghetti according to the package direction, reducing the cooking time by 1 minutes. It should be firm, but cooked.

- In a small bowl, mix together the Vegetable Broth, Oyster Sauce and Corn starch & set aside.

- Heat the Canola Oil in a medium wok, or chef's pan (a large frying pan can also be used) over high heat. Add the onions, celery and cabbage and stir fry for 2-3 minutes, or until the the cabbage begins to soften slightly. Add the cooked spaghetti, bean sprouts, carrots and garlic and continue to stir fry for another 2-3 minutes.

- Pour in the vegetable broth slurry, and stir fry for 1-2 minutes, or until the liquid thickens and clings to the pasta.

TABBOULEH - Serves 2 to 3

There are many variations of this cracked wheat salad that is
popular in the middle east. This dish can also be enjoyed as a
vegetarian meal by adding a cup of crumbled feta cheese.

NOTES:

TABBOULEH

Ingredients:

1 ½	cups	Cracked Wheat
1	pint	Grape Tomatoes
1	large	English Cucumber (seedless)
3	stalks	Green Onions
⅔	cup	Corn Oil
2	cloves	Garlic
½	bunch	Parsley (flat leaf)
¼	cup	Lemon Juice
½	teasp	Coriander (ground)
1	teasp	Salt
¼	teasp	Black Pepper

Method:

- Prepare the Cracked Wheat according to the package directions; for this recipe, #3 cracked wheat and boiling water was used and a ration of 1:1. It was covered with plastic wrap, in a medium glass bowl and left for 30 minutes; about 1 tablespoon of water was drained off.

- Cut the Grape Tomatoes in half and the Cucumber into thin, quarter moons, (about 1 ½ cups) and slice the Green Onion into thin slices. Mince the Garlic cloves.

- Finely mince the Parsley. There should be about ½ cup; most recipes are a lot "heavier" on this ingredient, so if that is your preference feel free to add as much as desired.

- Fluff the cooked wheat with a fork and add the Corn Oil. Stir until the kernels are well coated and not sticking together. Add in the grape tomatoes, cucumbers, green onion, garlic, parsley, Lemon Juice, Coriander, Salt & Pepper and stir until incorporated.

- Cover and chill for 1 hour, or more, in the refrigerator. Stir prior to serving.

RICE PILAF - Serves 2 to 3

A simply prepared rice & pasta dish that can be enjoyed as a main course or a side with other meat free fare.

NOTES:

RICE PILAF

Ingredients:

2	tablesp	Corn Oil
1	cup	Long Grain Rice
½	cup	Orzo
1	small	Red Onion
1	small	Yellow Onion
1	medium	Carrot
1	small	Red Bell Pepper
1	clove	Garlic
1	teasp	Oregano (dried)
½	teasp	Salt
⅛	teasp	Black Pepper
2 ¼ cups		Vegetable Broth
½	cup	Frozen Peas

Method:

- Finely dice the Red Onion, Yellow Onion, Carrot and Red Bell Pepper; there should be ½ cup of each. Mince the Garlic clove, or use a garlic press.

- In a medium frying pan (that has a tight fitting lid), heat the Corn Oil over medium heat. Add the Orzo, red & yellow onions and sauté for 5-7 minutes, or until the onions begin to soften.

- Add the garlic, Salt & Pepper and continue to cook, until the orzo begins to turn golden brown, about 3-4 minutes, stirring frequently.

- Stir in the Rice, carrot and Vegetable Broth, increase the heat to high and bring to a boil. Reduce heat to low, cover and simmer for 15 minutes, stirring occasionally.

- While the rice is cooking, place the Frozen Peas and red bell pepper in a colander, and rinse under warm running water until the peas have defrosted (3-4 minutes). Shake to drain excess water.

- Add them to the pan, stir and cook for an additional 5 minutes, covered, or until all of the liquid has been absorbed and the rice is cooked. Be sure to stir frequently to avoid burning the rice.

PASTA PUTTENESCA - Serves 2 to 3

This classic Italian pasta dish has a tangy taste from the olives and a bit of saltiness from the capers. It's a breeze to make, hearty and can be easily doubled to create 4-6 servings. Use any pasta variety that is available.

NOTES:

PASTA PUTTENESCA

Ingredients:

½	pound	Linguini
2	cloves	Garlic
¼	teasp	Red Pepper Flakes
1	tablesp	Canola Oil
1	can	Crushed Tomatoes (8 ounces)
¼	pound	Pitted Kalamata Olives (marinated)
¼	cup	Capers
½	teasp	Sugar
¼	teasp	Salt
1	teasp	Basil (dried)

Method:

- Cook the Linguini, according to package directions, drain and set aside. Rinse & wipe out the cooking pot to use for the sauce preparation.
- Mince the Garlic Cloves, or run through a press, rinse the Capers and set both aside. Taste a Kalamata Olive and if it is just too briny, quickly rinse them under cold water (about 15-20 seconds) to lessen the intensity of the flavor.
- Heat the pot over low heat, add the Canola Oil, garlic, Red Pepper Flakes and sauté for 1-2 minutes, or until fragrant. Be careful not to burn the garlic as it will make the entire dish taste bitter.
- Add the Crushed Tomatoes, olives, Capers, Sugar and Salt, stirring to combine. Increase the heat to medium, cover and cook for 2-3 minutes, or until the sauce begins to bubble.
- Stir in the cooked pasta and the Basil and toss until the sauce coats all of the linguini. Serve immediately.

COUS COUS - Serves 2 to 3

Cous Cous is not a grain, but rather a small pasta made from semolina flour. The addition of almonds and raisins makes this a sweet and savory dish that can be enjoyed, warm, at room temperature of even cold.

NOTES:

COUS COUS

Ingredients:

1	cup	Cous Cous (medium)
1	small	Zucchini
1	small	Red Onion
1	small	Carrot
1	clove	Garlic
½	cup	Slivered Almonds
2	tablesp	Canola Oil
1 ½	cups	Vegetable Broth
½	cup	Dark Raisins
½	teasp	Salt
⅛	teasp	Black Pepper
½	teasp	Oregano (dried)
½	teasp	Marjoram (dried)
½	teasp	Paprika

Method:

- Finely dice the Zucchini and Red Onion and slice the Carrot into thin disks; the yield should be about ½ cup of each. Mince the Garlic, or run through a garlic press.
- Heat a medium sized stock pot over medium-low heat. Add the Slivered Almonds and toast for 5-8 minutes, or until they begin to turn golden brown, tossing frequently to avoid burning. Remove from the pot and set aside.
- Return the pot to the stove, add the Canola Oil and increase the heat to medium-high. Add the zucchini, red onion, carrots, and garlic and sauté for 1-2 minutes, stirring frequently.
- Pour in the Vegetable Broth, Raisins, Salt, Pepper, Oregano, Marjoram and stir. Increase the heat to high and bring to a boil.
- Stir in the Cous Cous, remove from the heat, cover and allow to stand for 10-15 minutes, or until all of the broth has been absorbed. Try not to lift the lid too many times, as the trapped steam will help cook the cous cous.
- Sprinkle in the Paprika, stir and leave uncovered allowing the cous cous to cool to room temperature.

BROWN RICE & MUSHROOMS - Serves 3 to 4

The "chewy" texture and slightly "nutty" taste of brown rice add a different dimension to the easily prepared dish. The Cremini Mushrooms bring a much richer, deeper flavor than the white button variety.

NOTES:

BROWN RICE & MUSHROOMS

Ingredients:

2	cups	Brown Rice
8	ounces	Cremini Mushrooms
2	tablesp	Corn Oil
1	cloves	Garlic
4	cups	Vegetable Broth
1	teasp	Rosemary (dried)
½	teasp	Light Brown Sugar
⅛	teasp	Black Pepper

Method:

- Using a damp, clean kitchen towel, lightly wipe the tops of the Cremini Mushrooms clean. Remove the stems and cut into quarters. Mince the Garlic Clove.
- In a large stock pot, heat the Corn Oil over medium heat. Add the mushrooms and sauté for 5-7 minutes, or until they begin to release moisture and start to reduce in size.
- Stir in the Brown Rice and garlic and cook for 1-2 minutes, until the garlic become fragrant.
- Increase the heat to high and add the Vegetable Broth, Rosemary, Light Brown Sugar and Black Pepper, stir and bring to a boil.
- Reduce the heat to low, cover and cook for 35-40 minutes, or until the broth has been absorbed, stir occasionally.

STUFFED PEPPERS - Serves 3 to 4

A lighter take of the tomato sauce laden version you might be used to eating. The use of peppers that are cut in half, makes the oven baking time a bit shorter. Use any color of bell pepper for a different taste to the classic green.

NOTES:

STUFFED PEPPERS

Ingredients:

4	medium	Green Bell Peppers
1	cup	Long Grain White Rice
1	tablesp	Corn Oil
1	medium	Yellow Onion
2	medium	Carrots
2	cups	Vegetable Broth
1	can	Tomato Sauce (8 ounces)
1	teasp	Oregano (dried)
½	teasp	Basil (dried)
½	teasp	Garlic (granulated)
¼	teasp	Cinnamon (ground)
⅛	teasp	Black Pepper
¼	teasp	Salt

Method:

- Preheat oven to 375 degrees.
- Cut the Yellow Onion & Carrot into a small dice, to equal about ¾ cups of each.
- In a medium stock pot, heat the Corn Oil over medium heat and add the onion, carrot and White Rice and sauté for 5-7 minutes, or until the vegetables begin to soften. Stir in the Vegetable Broth, Tomato Sauce, Oregano, Basil, Garlic, Cinnamon, Salt and Black Pepper, increase heat to high and bring to a boil. Reduce heat the low, cover and cook for 12-15 minutes, or until the rice is cooked and the liquid has been absorbed.
- While the rice cooks, cut the Bell Peppers in half, length-wise and scoop out the seeds and white ribs, taking care not to rip them apart. Check that each half can lie flat with the cut side up; use a vegetable peeler to take a small slice off of the back if needed. Place the peppers in a shallow baking dish.
- Once the rice has cooked, remove from heat. Fill each pepper half with about ½ cup of rice, there should be just enough to divide equally among 8 halves; of course this will depend on the size the peppers used.
- Fill the baking dish with water to ¼ inch high, cover, place on the center rack in the oven and bake for 30-40 minutes, or until the peppers have softened, but are not falling apart.

KASHA - Serves 3 to 4

This whole grain (roasted buckwheat groats), is generally prepared with eggs and/or chicken fat, as a porridge or stuffing for knish, stands up well on its own, as a hearty vegan main course meal.

NOTES:

KASHA

Ingredients:

1 ½	cups	Kasha
1	cup	Shelled Walnuts
1	large	Vidalia Onion
2	cloves	Garlic
2	tablesp	Corn Oil
½	teasp	Salt
¼	teasp	Black Pepper
1	teasp	Thyme (dried)
¼	teasp	All Spice (ground)
3	cups	Vegetable Broth

Method:

- In a small pot, blanch the Walnuts in boiling water for 5-7 minutes, or until they begin to lose color and soften. Drain and set aside.

- Cut the Vidalia Onion into a medium dice to equal about 1 ½ cups. Mince the Garlic Cloves.

- In a medium stock pot, dry roast the Kasha, over medium-low heat for 3-4 minutes. Remove and set aside.

- Return the pot to the stove, and heat the Corn Oil over medium heat; add the onion, garlic, Salt, Black Pepper, Thyme and All Spice and sauté for 3-4 minutes, or until the onions soften and the garlic becomes fragrant.

- Stir in the kasha, walnuts and Vegetable Broth and bring the mixture to a boil. Reduce the heat to low, cover and cook for 10-15 minutes, or until most of the liquid is absorbed. Remove from heat, keep covered and let stand for 10-12 minutes, or until all of the broth has been absorbed.

PUERTO RICAN RICE - Serves 3 to 4

A classic Puerto Rican rice dish, made vegan by removing the traditional pork ingredients. The turmeric provides a deep, rich yellow color, so it's optional. Serve with warm tortillas and top with your favorite hot sauce if desired.

NOTES:

PUERTO RICAN RICE

Ingredients:

1 ½	cups	Long Grain White Rice
1	small	Poblano Pepper
1	small	Cubanelle Pepper
1	medium	Yellow Onion
2	cloves	Garlic
1	medium	Plum Tomato
¼	bunch	Cilantro
1	teasp	Oregano (dried)
1	teasp	Paprika
½	teasp	Coriander (ground)
¼	teasp	Turmeric (ground)
½	teasp	Salt
⅛	teasp	Black Pepper
1	can	Pigeon Peas (15 ounces)
½	cup	Stuffed Spanish Olives

Method:

- Cut the Poblano & Cubanelle peppers in half, lengthwise, remove the seeds and white ribs, and then into a fine dice, about ¼ cup each. Cut the Yellow Onion & Tomato into a small dice, equaling about ½ cup each. Mince the Garlic, or run through a press. Mince the Cilantro to equal about ¼ cup. Darin & rinse the Pigeon Peas.

- In a large skillet, heat the Corn Oil over medium heat. Add the peppers, onion, tomato, garlic & Oregano and sauté for 4-5 minutes, or until the vegetables begin to soften.

- Add the Rice, Paprika, Coriander, Turmeric, Salt and Black Pepper and stir to coat. Increase the heat to high, pour in the Vegetable Broth, and the cilantro, stir frequently until the mixture comes to a boil. Cover and reduce the heat to low; cook for 8-10 minutes, or until most of the liquid is absorbed.

- Add the pigeon peas and the Stuffed Olives, stir, cover and continue to cook for 4-5 minutes, or until all of the liquid is absorbed and the peas have heated through.

SEAFOOD DISHES

HATTERAS CLAM CHOWDER

SHRIMP AND GRITS

BAY SCALLOP STIR FRY

LOBSTER RISOTTO

PALM SUNDAY FISH

HATTERAS CLAM CHOWDER - Serves 2 to 3

This soup is a bit different than the classic New England & Manhattan style chowders that most people are familiar with, but just as hearty. The minimal ingredients provide for a simple and quick preparation.

NOTES:

HATTERAS CLAM CHOWDER

Ingredients:

2	cans	Minced Clams (6.5 ounces each)
8	ounces	Clam Juice
2	medium	White Potatoes (about 1.5 pounds total)
1	medium	Yellow Onions
3	medium	Carrots
3	stalks	Celery
1	clove	Garlic
1	tablesp	Corn Oil
2	cups	Vegetable Broth
½	teasp	Thyme (dried)
½	teasp	Marjoram (dried)
1	each	Bay Leaf

Method:

- Cut the Onion and Celery into a small dice to equal about 1 cup each. Cut the Carrots in half lengthwise, and then slice into half moons to equal about 1 cup. Peel the potatoes and then cut into ½ inch cubes; there should be about 3 ½ cups. Mince the Garlic Clove. Drain the Minced Clams, but do not rinse them.

- In a medium stock pot, heat the Corn Oil over medium heat. Add the onions, celery, garlic, Thyme & Marjoram and sauté for 3-5 minutes, or until the vegetables begin to soften.

- Add the potatoes, carrots, clams, Clam Juice, Bay Leaf and Vegetable Broth. Increase the heat to high, and bring to a boil. Reduce heat to low and simmer, covered for 15-20 minutes, or until the potatoes are tender. Remove the bay leaf before serving.

SHRIMP AND GRITS - Serves 3 to 4

A New Orleans favorite that is surprisingly easy to make and satisfies every time. Any size of cooked shrimp can be used (30/40, in this recipe) and a teaspoon or two of red pepper sauce can be added to taste, for a bit of a kick.

NOTES:

SHRIMP AND GRITS

Ingredients:

¾	cups	Grits (Quaker® 5 minute instant)
½	teasp	Garlic (granulated)
½	teasp	Salt (divided)
1	small	Yellow Onion
1	small	Green Bell Pepper
1	clove	Garlic
2	tablesp	Canola Oil
⅔	cup	Tomato Juice
2	tablesp	Lemon Juice
½	teasp	Paprika
¼	teasp	Cumin (ground)
⅛	teasp	Black Pepper
¼	bunch	Parsley (curly)
1	pound	Frozen Shrimp (cooked, peeled, tail-on)

Method:

- Cut the Yellow Onion and Green Bell Pepper into a fine dice, equaling about ¼ cup of each. Mince the Parsley to equal about 2-3 tablespoons. Mince the Garlic Clove.

- Defrost the Frozen Shrimp, in a colander, under cold running water, for 7-10 minutes. Drain them thoroughly & pat dry.

- Cook the Grits according to package directions, using 3 cups of water and adding the Granulated Garlic and ¼ teaspoon of Salt. Cover and keep warm over very low heat.

- In a medium skillet, heat the Canola Oil over medium heat and add the onions, green pepper and garlic and cook for 3-4 minutes, or until they begin to soften, stirring frequently.

- Add the Tomato Juice, Lemon Juice, Paprika, Cumin, ¼ teaspoon of Salt and stir to combine. Increase the heat to medium-high & cook for 2-3 minutes, allowing the sauce to thicken slightly.

- Stir in the shrimp and parsley and continue to cook until the shrimp is heated through, about 2-3 minutes. Serve over the prepared grits.

BAY SCALLOP STIR FRY - Serves 2 to 3

This is a lighter stir fry that does not have soy sauce. The bay scallops should be available, frozen, at your local market and are relatively inexpensive compared to the larger sea scallops.

NOTES:

BAY SCALLOP STIR FRY

Ingredients:

1	pound	Bay Scallops (frozen)
½	pound	Snow Peas (fresh)
2	medium	Yellow Bell Peppers
½	pound	White Button Mushrooms
2	cloves	Garlic
½	cup	Vegetable Broth
1	teasp	Ginger (ground)
1	teasp	Lemon Juice
½	teasp	Sugar
1	tablesp	Corn Starch
2	tablesp	Corn Oil (divided)

Method:

- Trim the stem, or string end, of the Snow Peas. Cut the Yellow Bell Pepper into ½ inch pieces. Remove the stems from the Mushrooms, peel the caps and cut into quarters. Mince the Garlic, or run through a garlic press.

- In a small bowl, whisk together The Vegetable Broth, Ginger, Lemon Juice, Sugar and Corn Starch and set aside.

- Defrost the Bay Scallops under cool running water and pat dry, or follow the package directions and pat dry. The less moisture that is released by the scallops during their cooking stage, the better.

- Heat a wok, or large chef's pan over high heat. Once the pan is hot, add 1 tablespoon of Corn Oil, the Snow Peas, Bell Pepper, Mushrooms and Garlic and stir fry for 2-3 minutes, or until the mushrooms begin to soften and lose volume. Remove and set aside.

- Wipe out the pan with a clean kitchen towel and place back over the heat. Once the pan gets hot again, add the remaining tablespoon of the Corn Oil and then the scallops. Stir fry for 1-2 minutes, or until they are almost cooked. Put the vegetables back in, and add the vegetable broth "slurry" and continue to stir fry until the sauce thickens and the scallops are fully cooked, about 1-2 minutes. Serve with rice, if desired.

LOBSTER RISOTTO - Serves 3 to 4

This Italian dish has many variations, such as this one with lobster. The key is constantly stirring during the cooking process, but the reward is a creamy and flavorful rice. Cooked shrimp will work just as well.

NOTES:

LOBSTER RISOTTO

Ingredients:

2	each	Frozen Lobster Tails (4 ounces each)
6	cups	Vegetable Broth
1	small	Shallot
1	clove	Garlic
1	small	Red Bell Pepper
1 ½	cups	Arborio Rice
1	tablesp	Canola Oil

Method:

- Using broth cubes for this recipe is not recommended. During the lobster cooking stage, it reduces to a saltier liquid. Please use canned or carton broth for this preparation, or cook the lobster separately if you are using cubes.

- Finely dice the Red Bell Pepper to equal about ⅓ cup. Mince the Garlic, or run through a press. Mince the Shallot to equal about 2 tablespoons.

- Bring the Vegetable Stock to a boil in a medium pot. Rinse the Lobster Tails under cold running water for 30 seconds and place in the boiling broth. Cook the tails until done. Approximately 8-10 minutes, or until the shells turn bright red and the meat in tender, when poked with a toothpick. Remove the tails from the broth (do not pour out the broth) and rinse under cold running water for 1-2 minutes, or until cool enough to handle. Remove all of the tail meat, cut into ¼ pieces and set aside.

- In a chef's pan, or skillet, heat the Canola Oil over medium heat. Add the Arborio Rice, shallot and garlic and sauté for 1-2 minutes, or until it becomes fragrant.

- Add the broth, ½ cup at a time and stir until the liquid is absorbed.. Continue to add broth, ½ cup at a time, stirring until the broth is absorbed. When you reach the last ½ cup the rice will have expanded 2-3 times its original size and it should have a creamy texture. Add the last of the broth and stir until there is just a bit left and remove from heat.

- Fold in the red bell pepper & lobster and let stand for 2-3 minutes. Stir and serve.

PALM SUNDAY FISH - Serves 3 to 4

If you cannot attend your local parish for the traditional after service luncheon, or want to have fried fish for dinner here is a recipe that is easy to prepare. The key here is using fresh fish; if using frozen (defrosted) be sure to squeeze out excess water.

NOTES:

PALM SUNDAY FISH

Ingredients:

2	pounds	Cod
½	cup	All Purpose Flour
2	tablesp	Corn Starch
1	teasp	Baking Powder
½	teasp	Salt
½	teasp	Garlic (granulated)
½	teasp	Onion (granulated)
¾	cup	Club Soda
1	tablesp	Corn Oil
3	cups	Panko Bread Crumbs
2	cups	Corn Oil – for frying

Method:

- Cut the Cod into 4 ounces fillets, or have the fish monger at the market do this; pieces used for this recipe were about 3 inches long, 2 inches wide and about ½ inch thick. Rinse and pat dry.
- Combine the Flour, Corn Starch, Baking Powder, Salt, Garlic and Onion in a bowl and stir until well combined. Whisk in the Club Soda and the tablespoon of Corn Oil until smooth.
- Heat the Corn Oil (for frying) in a medium skillet over medium heat (a 9" non-stick was used for the preparation).
- Pour half of the Panko Bread Crumbs into a shallow plate.
- When the oil comes up to temperature, dip the fillets (two at a time) into the batter mixture, shake off the excess, and place in the bread crumbs and coat both sides.
- Fry the fillets for 2-3 minutes per side, or until the coating turns golden brown. Of course the total cooking time depends on the thickness of each fillet.

VEGAN DESSERTS

PUMPKIN MOUSSE

APPLE ROLL-UPS

BANANAS FOSTER

BLUBERRY CRUMBLE

RICE CEREAL BARS

POACHED PEARS

PUMPKIN MOUSSE - Serves 3 to 4

Here is a simple, three ingredient dessert that you can be prepared in no time. Substituting cold water, for milk, makes it a vegan "treat" to enjoy after any meal.

NOTES:

PUMPKIN MOUSSE

Ingredients:

1	can	Pure Pumpkin (15 ounces)
2	packages	Jell-O® French Vanilla Pudding Mix (3.4 oz each)
½	teasp	Vanilla Extract

Method:

- Pour ½ cup of water into measuring cup with 2-3 ice cubes.
- Add the Pumpkin to a mixing bowl and beat with a hand blender, at medium speed, for 5-7 minutes, or until it becomes smooth.
- Remove the ice cubes from the water, pour it into the bowl along with the Pudding Mix and continue to beating for 7-10 minutes, or until the mixture is creamy. Add cold water a tablespoon at a time, if needed.
- Refrigerate for at least 15 minutes before serving.

APPLE ROLL-UPS - Serves 5 to 6

Hand held "apple pie" that takes a little work, but taste great.
Any variety of apple will work fine in this recipe, along with dark
raisins.

NOTES:

APPLE ROLL-UPS

Ingredients:

2	small	Granny Smith Apples
2	small	Golden Delicious Apples
½	cup	Golden Raisins
¼	cup	Apple Sauce
¼	cup	Dark Brown Sugar
¼	teasp	Cinnamon (ground)
½	teasp	Salt
1	tablesp	Canola Oil
6	each	Flour Tortillas

Method:

- Preheat oven to 375 degrees. Line a baking sheet with foil and spray lightly with cooking spray.
- Place the Golden Raisins in a small boil and add 1 cup of boiling water. Cover with plastic wrap and set aside.
- Core, peel and dice the Granny Smith & Golden Delicious Apples into a small dice. There should be a total of 2 cups of each.
- In a medium frying pan, heat the Canola Oil over medium heat and add the apples & Salt. Sauté for 15-20 minutes, or until they begin to soften.
- Add the Apple Sauce, Brown Sugar and Cinnamon, stir until combined and continue to cook for 8-10 minutes, or until the mixture has tightened and there is little moisture, stirring frequently. Remove from heat and allow to cool for 5 minutes.
- Heat the Flour Tortillas in the microwave for 1 minutes at 40%, or until they soften and become pliable. Fill each tortilla, down the middle, with about 3 tablespoons of the apple filling, fold both ends over and place seam side down on the cookie sheet.
- Spray each roll-up lightly with cooking spray. Bake on the center rake for 30-35 minutes, or until they begin to turn golden brown.

BANANAS FOSTER - Serves 2 to 3

Traditionally made with dark rum, butter and served over ice cream, this vegan preparation is a great alternative.

NOTES:

BANANAS FOSTER

Ingredients:

3	medium	Ripe Bananas
1	cup	Dark Brown Sugar
¾	cup	Shelled Walnuts
2	tablesp	Corn Oil
¼	teasp	Cinnamon
⅛	teasp	Salt
½	teasp	Vanilla Extract

Method:

- Peel the Bananas and cut into 1 inch long pieces.
- Combine the Corn Oil, Brown Sugar and ¼ cup Water in a medium, non-stick skillet until dissolved. Place the pan over medium –low heat and cook for 3-4 minutes, stirring frequently.
- Add the Walnuts, Cinnamon, and Salt and cook for 7-10 minutes, or until the sauce has reduced by half and has the consistency of honey.
- Add the bananas and Vanilla Extract, mix well to coat the fruit. Continue cooking for 2-3 minutes, or until the bananas have softened slightly.
- Allow to cool for 5-10 minutes before serving.

BLUEBERRY CRUMBLE - Serves 2 to 3

This dessert is not too sweet or too tart and surprisingly simple to make. Using readily available frozen blueberries and few basic crumble ingredients makes it a good go to in a pinch.

NOTES:

BLUEBERRY CRUMBLE

Ingredients:

4	cups	Frozen Blueberries
1	tablesp	Corn Starch
⅔	cup	Rolled Oats
2	tablesp	All Purpose Flour
3	tablesp	Brown Sugar
¼	teasp	Salt
2	tablesp	Canola Oil

Method:

- Preheat the oven to 375 degrees. Lightly coat an 8" x 8" glass baking dish with cooking spray.
- In a medium bowl, mix the Frozen Blueberries and Cornstarch until well combined. Spread the blueberries evenly in the prepared baking dish.
- Place the Rolled Oats, Brown Sugar and Salt in a small bowl and mix until combined. Break up any lumps of brown sugar using the back of a fork or your fingers. Pour in the Canola Oil and mix with a fork to evenly distribute the oil. Continue to mix until the topping texture is coarse and mealy. Spread evenly on top of the blueberries.
- Place the dish in the oven, on the center rack and bake for 30-35 minutes, uncovered, or until the juices begin to bubble along the sides.
- Cool slightly before serving.

CEREAL BARS - Serves 4 to 5

An update to this dessert staple using corn oil in place of butter. The combination of the cocoa flavored cereal and peanut butter make this just plain yummy!

NOTES:

CRISPY RICE CEREAL BARS

Ingredients:

2 ½	cups	Crispy Rice Cereal (cocoa flavored)
22	large	Marshmallows
⅓	cup	Creamy Peanut Butter
2	tablesp	Corn Oil
½	teasp	Vanilla Extract

Method:

- Lightly spray a 9" x 5" non-stick bread pan with cooking spray.
- In a medium non-stick stock pot, heat the Corn Oil over low heat. Add the Marshmallows, stir to combine with the oil and cook for 4-5 minutes, or until melted. Remove from heat.
- Stir in the Peanut Butter and Vanilla Extract until smooth. Add the Crispy Rice Cereal and stir until well combined.
- Using a rubber spatula, spread the mixture evenly in the bread pan. Allow to cool at room temperature for a few hours. Remove from the pan and slice into 6 bars.

Made in the USA
Charleston, SC
24 August 2013